THE OFFICIAL
ENGLAND RUGBY
ANNUAL 2025

Written by Calum McLaggan
Designed by Dan Brawn

A Grange Publication

© 2024. Published by Grange Communications Ltd., Edinburgh, under licence from England Rugby. Printed in the EU.

Photographs © England Rugby and Alamy

ISBN: 978-1-915879-84-4

CONTENTS

06 Welcome

07 2024/25 Fixtures

08 Countdown to Rugby World Cup 2025

10 Rugby World Cup 2025 Stadium Guide

12 Bronze In France

14 Player Profile: Ben Earl

15 Player Profile: Marcus Smith

16 Wordsearch

17 Quiz: Who Am I?

18 Men's Six Nations Review

20 England's Rising Stars

22 Red Roses: Did You Know?

24 Women's Six Nations Review

26 Red Roses Fans

27 Mission: Fill Allianz Stadium

28 Quiz: Spot The Difference

29 Quiz: Guess the Player with Emojis

30 World At Her Feet

32 Meg and Ellie's Olympic Dreams

34 Men's Summer Series Review

36 Premiership Women's Rugby Champions

37 Premiership Champions

38 Joe Marler's Bizarre Assist

39 Quiz: Spot The Ball

40
Grassroots
Heroes

42
Introducing
T1 Rugby

44
RWC 2025 in
Numbers

46
2023/24
Results Recap

48
Men's Player
Profiles

54
Women's Player
Profiles

60
Quiz Answers

WELCOME

What a year it's been, England Rugby fans.

If you enjoyed the thrills and spills of the 2023/24 season, from the Rugby World Cup to the Six Nations and everything in between, here's some good news: we're about to do it all again in 2025.

Before you dive into our annual, though, grab a pen and ring 22 August in your calendar: it's when England kick off the 2025 Women's Rugby World Cup and the start of six epic weeks of rugby on home soil.

The Red Roses have been in irresistible form of late, securing a third straight Grand Slam in the 2024 Women's Six Nations, and we'll be backing them to go all the way at the Rugby World Cup.

England Men went from strength to strength in 2024, with victories over Italy, Wales, and Ireland in the Six Nations, and impressive performances against Japan and New Zealand in the Summer Series.

Next up for Steve Borthwick's men: four highly anticipated home matches this November, including a showdown against the world champions, South Africa, on 16 November.

So, what are you waiting for? Let's dive right in and go on an England Rugby adventure together!

2024/25 FIXTURES

MEN'S AUTUMN INTERNATIONALS 2024

ENGLAND V NEW ZEALAND
Saturday 2 November at 15:10
ALLIANZ STADIUM

ENGLAND V AUSTRALIA
Saturday 9 November at 15:10
ALLIANZ STADIUM

ENGLAND V SOUTH AFRICA
Saturday 16 November at 17:40
ALLIANZ STADIUM

ENGLAND V JAPAN
Sunday 24 November at 16:10
ALLIANZ STADIUM

MEN'S SIX NATIONS 2025

IRELAND V ENGLAND
Saturday 1 February at 16:45
AVIVA STADIUM

ENGLAND V FRANCE
Saturday 8 February at 16:45
ALLIANZ STADIUM

ENGLAND V SCOTLAND
Saturday 22 February at 16:45
ALLIANZ STADIUM

ENGLAND V ITALY
Sunday 9 March at 15:00
ALLIANZ STADIUM

WALES V ENGLAND
Saturday 15 March at 16:45
PRINCIPALITY STADIUM

WOMEN'S AUTUMN INTERNATIONALS 2024

ENGLAND V FRANCE
Saturday 7 September at 14:30
KINGSHOLM STADIUM

ENGLAND V NEW ZEALAND
Saturday 14 September at 14:30
ALLIANZ STADIUM

WXV 2024 - CANADA

USA V ENGLAND
Sunday 29 September at 20:30
BC PLACE

NEW ZEALAND V ENGLAND
Sunday 6 October at 21:00
LANGLEY EVENTS CENTRE

CANADA V ENGLAND
Sunday 13 October at 03:00
BC PLACE

KEEP AN EYE OUT ON ENGLANDRUGBY.COM FOR THE 2025 WOMEN'S SIX NATIONS FIXTURES

*Schedule not confirmed at time of printing

RED ROSES COUNTDOWN TO RUGBY WORLD CUP 2025

Between 22 August and 27 September, the 16 best women's teams in the world will arrive in England for Rugby World Cup 2025. It will be a historic time for women's rugby, with the Red Roses ready to inspire England's next generation of players and fans.

This will be the 10th Women's Rugby World Cup. England have won the game's biggest prize twice and have finished runners-up on six occasions, including a heart-breaking defeat last time out against the Black Ferns in 2021. We'll all be hoping the Red Roses can go one step further this time, and, if current form is anything to go by, there are plenty of reasons to be optimistic about their chances in 2025.

PAST WINNERS AND RUNNERS-UP

Year	Winners	Runners-up
1991	USA	England
1994	England	USA
1998	New Zealand	USA
2002	New Zealand	England
2006	New Zealand	England
2010	New Zealand	England
2014	England	Canada
2017	New Zealand	England
2021	New Zealand	England

As the host nation, the Red Roses will kick off the action under the Friday night lights at Sunderland's Stadium of Light, with the final set to take place five weeks later at the home of English rugby, Allianz Stadium.

CHECK OUT THE FULL LIST OF VENUES ON THE NEXT PAGE

STADIUM GUIDE

Fans across the country will get the chance to see the world's best in action, with eight cities set to host matches at the tournament. From the South West to the North East via the biggest rugby stadium in the world, here are the eight host venues for Rugby World Cup 2025.

Manchester
SALFORD COMMUNITY STADIUM
11,404

Bristol
ASHTON GATE
26,387

Exeter
SANDY PARK
15,000

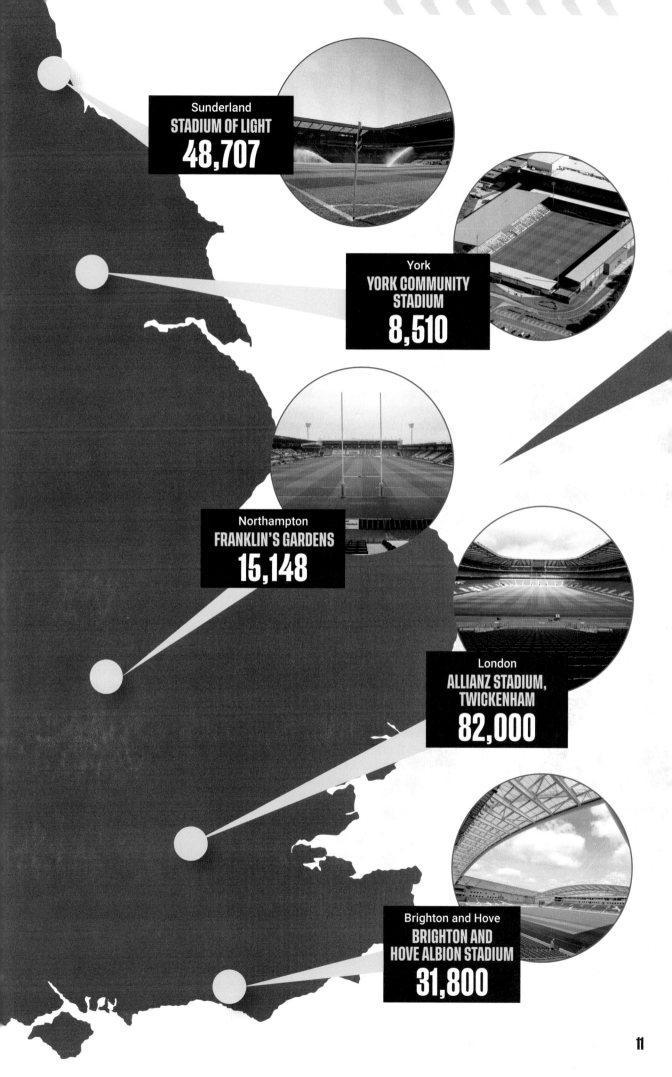

Sunderland
STADIUM OF LIGHT
48,707

York
YORK COMMUNITY STADIUM
8,510

Northampton
FRANKLIN'S GARDENS
15,148

London
ALLIANZ STADIUM, TWICKENHAM
82,000

Brighton and Hove
BRIGHTON AND HOVE ALBION STADIUM
31,800

England Rugby

BRONZE IN FRANCE

RWC 2023 REVIEW

Exciting. Nailbiting. Exhilarating. Heartbreaking.

England finished third at Rugby World Cup 2023, and – as any England fan will remember – it was a tournament packed with unforgettable moments. One thing's for sure: Steve Borthwick's men can be more than proud of what they achieved. Here's a look back at England's path to a bronze medal finish in France.

ENGLAND 27-10 ARGENTINA

England got their campaign off to a dream start in Marseille, with George Ford slotting six penalties and three drop goals en route to a much needed victory against Argentina, despite going a man down after just three minutes!

ENGLAND 71-0 CHILE

England then made the trip north to Lille for their last two Pool D matches. Against Chile, England ran in 11 tries in a thumping win against Los Cóndores, including five from 20-year-old Henry Arundell in his first outing at the tournament.

ENGLAND 34-12 JAPAN

Next up, England faced Japan, and ran in four tries to clinch a bonus-point win in Nice. Lewis Ludlam, Courtney Lawes, Freddie Steward and Joe Marchant all crossed for England, with Steward's spectacular aerial take from George Ford's cross-kick the pick of the bunch.

ENGLAND 18-17 SAMOA

Then came a knife-edged match against Samoa, who pushed England all the way and could have won. The decisive moment eventually came from a familiar source, Danny Care, who darted over from the base of a scrum in the 73rd minute to help steer England to nerve-racking win.

INTO THE KNOCK-OUT STAGES WITH FOUR WINS FROM FOUR!

POOL D STANDINGS

	P	W	L	D	Pts Diff	Bonus	Pts
England	4	4	0	0	111	2	18
Argentina	4	3	1	0	58	2	14
Japan	4	2	2	0	2	1	9
Samoa	4	1	3	0	17	3	7
Chile	4	0	4	0	-188	0	0

QUARTER FINAL   ENGLAND 30-24 FIJI

England started brightly against Fiji, with Manu Tuilagi and Joe Marchant getting on the scoresheet in the first half and Owen Farrell's pinpoint kicking giving England a 21-10 lead at the break. Fiji left it late but exploded into life with two converted tries in four minutes to draw the scores level, and it came down to Owen Farrell to rescue the day with a late drop goal and a penalty as England held out for the win.

SEMI FINAL   ENGLAND 15-16 SOUTH AFRICA

Steve Borthwick's men came close to an almighty upset against the reigning champions but fell short despite a brave performance against the eventual Rugby World Cup winners. Owen Farrell was again on top form from the tee, slotting four penalties and a drop goal as England led for most of the match. But a late South Africa try followed by a monster penalty from Handré Pollard saw the Springboks seal their spot in the final by the narrowest of margins.

BRONZE FINAL   ENGLAND 26-23 ARGENTINA

Time for one last push and a rematch against Argentina in Paris. England turned on the style early on at the Stade de France with Ben Earl scoring inside 10 minutes and Theo Dan bursting over the line after a neat link-up with Marcus Smith. Argentina worked their way back into the game in the second half, but a dogged England held out to clinch the win and, with it, the bronze medal at Rugby World Cup 2023.

TOP WORK, BOYS.

PLAYER PROFILE
BEN EARL

When it comes to describing Ben Earl, England teammate Ollie Chessum summed it up perfectly: "It's definitely better playing with him than against him."

The Saracens and England No. 8 enjoyed arguably the best season of his career in 2023/24, picking up a Player of the Championship nomination after a stand-out series of performances in the Six Nations.

The stats don't lie either. Ben finished the tournament ranked first for carries [72] and gain line breaks [31], and second for defenders beaten [24] and contact metres [86].

"

HE'S OUTSTANDING. WE NEED THREE OR FOUR PEOPLE LIKE HIM.

Former England No. 8
Dean Richards on Ben Earl.

England
Rugby

PLAYER PROFILE
MARCUS SMITH

It took less than a year for Marcus Smith to go from captaining Brighton College to getting involved in the England squad, and the Harlequins fly half's rapid rise shows no signs of slowing down.

Marcus made his England debut against the USA in 2021, and a Lions call-up quickly followed. But it wasn't exactly a conventional call-up. He was selected as an injury replacement for Finn Russell while playing for England against Canada and was given the news after being substituted late on in the game. Imagine the surprise!

Since then, the mercurial 10 has gone on to win over 30 England caps, racking up 12 tries and 200 points. Watch this space: there's plenty more to come from one of the most exciting fly halves in world rugby.

"

I THOUGHT I WAS BEING TOLD OFF OR HAD DONE SOMETHING WRONG!

Marcus Smith on his surprise Lions call-up after being substituted.

THE AMAZING RUGBY WORDSEARCH

PUT YOUR DETECTIVE SKILLS TO THE TEST WITH OUR RUGBY WORD SEARCH.

CAN YOU FIND ALL 20 RUGBY TERMS IN THE GRID BELOW? WORDS CAN GO HORIZONTALLY, VERTICALLY, AND DIAGONALLY IN ALL DIRECTIONS. GOOD LUCK!

Y	F	H	K	D	L	L	A	D	N	A	R	Y	R	R	A	H	R
A	L	L	I	A	N	Z	S	T	A	D	I	U	M	L	K	G	O
Y	S	I	X	N	A	T	I	O	N	S	E	A	X	A	T	L	F
B	Z	F	L	U	D	F	I	T	O	R	S	L	J	N	L	S	F
Q	R	O	M	A	U	D	M	U	I	R	F	L	D	I	S	E	S
T	E	E	L	M	O	F	I	X	R	E	S	I	E	F	B	U	I
M	C	R	D	E	V	G	R	A	A	I	T	L	B	I	O	E	D
A	T	H	K	R	T	Y	P	E	S	E	A	S	M	M	N	I	E
S	I	D	L	U	O	I	R	O	D	W	D	T	N	E	U	M	P
C	A	N	E	B	H	S	O	T	R	D	I	A	N	S	S	I	L
O	J	A	L	A	O	D	E	E	A	D	U	D	P	U	P	V	S
T	X	L	Z	C	T	G	N	A	T	U	M	I	O	X	O	I	E
H	A	R	T	W	I	C	M	E	R	H	E	E	D	B	I	N	N
B	V	E	R	L	E	A	R	T	Y	T	V	R	I	P	N	Q	O
S	I	D	O	F	B	M	A	R	C	U	S	S	M	I	T	H	J
K	E	N	P	C	E	R	H	B	E	B	A	F	H	G	I	B	G
A	R	U	H	L	M	A	X	B	M	E	J	N	U	B	E	S	E
T	O	S	Y	E	L	O	C	N	A	D	G	J	K	G	E	T	M

SIX NATIONS	OFFSIDE	DEBUT
BALLBOY	BONUS POINT	RED ROSE
DROP GOAL	HARRY RANDALL	TEE
SEMI FINAL	SUNDERLAND	TROPHY
MARCUS SMITH	ALLIANZ STADIUM	
MASCOT	TRY	
DAN COLE	MAUD MUIR	**ANSWERS ON PAGE 60**
OLLIE LAWRENCE	MEG JONES	

WHO AM I?

THINK YOU KNOW ENGLAND'S STARS? LET'S PUT YOUR KNOWLEDGE TO THE TEST.

SEE IF YOU CAN IDENTIFY THIS ENGLAND REGULAR FROM THE CLUES BELOW...

FACT 1
I MADE MY PROFESSIONAL DEBUT FOR SALE SHARKS IN 2016.

FACT 2
WHEN I MADE MY INTERNATIONAL DEBUT IN 2017, I BECAME THE YOUNGEST FORWARD TO PLAY FOR ENGLAND SINCE 1912.

FACT 3
TALKING OF WHICH, I WAS ALSO THE YOUNGEST PLAYER IN ENGLAND'S 2019 RUGBY WORLD CUP SQUAD.

FACT 4
I WAS NOMINATED FOR THE WORLD RUGBY PLAYER OF THE YEAR AWARD LATER THAT YEAR.

FACT 5
I HAVE A TWIN BROTHER CALLED BEN.

FACT 6
MY SURNAME IS ALSO THE NAME OF A POPULAR TYPE OF FOOD FROM INDIA.

STILL NOT SURE?
CHECK OUT THE ANSWER ON PAGE 60

17

FINE MARGINS
IN THE SIX NATIONS

Take a look back at an 'edge of the seat' Six Nations campaign, with all five matches decided by single-point margins, as England won three from five to finish third.

ITALY 24 – 27 ENGLAND

First up: a tricky opener against an ever-improving Italy side at the Stadio Olimpico. The Azzurri burst into an early 10-point lead, but England fought back with tries from Elliot Daly and Alex Mitchell, while the ever-reliable George Ford racked up 17 points from the tee.

The match provided an excellent opportunity to introduce new boys like Fin Smith and Immanuel Feyi-Waboso to international rugby, and another England debutant, Ethan Roots, even picked up the Man of the Match Award.

ENGLAND 16 – 14 WALES

England made it two from two with a narrow victory against Wales at Allianz Stadium , but, as the scoreline suggests, it was another hard-fought contest between two great rivals. A far-from-perfect start saw Wales find themselves 7 points and two men up after 17 minutes, but a Ben Earl try got England up and running soon after.

England came out firing after the restart, and the breakthrough eventually came with an hour on the clock when Fraser Dingwall dived over in the corner to score his first-ever try at Allianz Stadium to bring England within a point: imagine how that would have felt! Then, with 10 minutes to go, George Ford slotted a penalty to edge England in front for the first time in the match as the hosts held out to clinch a narrow win.

> **"**
> ## IT'S PRETTY SURREAL. WORDS CANNOT DESCRIBE IT; IT'S VERY SPECIAL.
>
> Ethan Roots on winning the MOTM Award on his England debut.

SCOTLAND 30 – 21 ENGLAND

On to Edinburgh to face Scotland and a chance to reclaim the Calcutta Cup for the first time in four years. England made a blistering start, with George Furbank finishing off a well-worked set piece inside five minutes and George Ford adding three points from the tee.

Scotland rallied well, though, with Finn Russell putting in a laser-sharp performance from the tee and Duhan van der Merwe scoring a hat-trick. Imanuel Feyi-Waboso gave England a glimmer of hope with a 67th minute score, but it wasn't enough to take the spoils at Murrayfield.

ENGLAND 23 - 22 IRELAND

Best way to get the campaign back on track? How about a win against the reigning Grand Slam champions? Ollie Lawrence got England off to a dream start with a brilliant score inside 5 minutes, but the men in green responded with four Jack Crowley penalties and a James Lowe try.

England exploded into life after the restart, taking the lead with tries from George Furbank and Ben Earl, before Lowe's second with seven minutes left on the clock saw the visitors edge back in front. The decisive moment came with the clock in the red, and Ireland pinned on their line when Marcus Smith dropped back and slotted a match-winning drop goal to clinch a famous win and send the Allianz Stadium crowd into raptures. What a moment!

FRANCE 33 - 31 ENGLAND

On to Lyon for Le Crunch and what would turn out to be the game of the 2024 Six Nations championship as France and England played out a seven-try thriller. The hosts put in a big first-half performance, lit up by Le Garrec's coast-to-coast try, but Ollie Lawrence's score just before the break kick-started England's fightback as Steve Borthwick's men scored an amazing 21 unanswered points in just seven minutes of play.

France rallied with two tries in quick succession, but when Tommy Freeman glided over in the corner, and George Ford slotted a stunning touchline conversion to take the score to 31-30 with five minutes to play, England seemed to be on course for victory. But, with seconds left on the clock, France won a penalty on the halfway line, which Thomas Ramos somehow managed to send through the uprights from 50 metres out to rescue a late win for Les Bleus.

"

CREDIT TO SCOTLAND FOR A REALLY STRONG PERFORMANCE. THEY'RE A TEAM THAT HAVE BEEN TOGETHER FOR A NUMBER OF YEARS, WHILE WE'RE STILL TRYING TO DEVELOP.

Steve Borthwick on Scotland v England

FINAL STANDINGS

	P	W	L	D	Pts Diff	Bonus	Pts
Ireland	5	4	1	0	84	4	20
France	5	3	1	1	6	1	15
England	5	3	2	0	-5	2	14
Scotland	5	2	3	0	0	4	12
Italy	5	2	2	1	-34	1	11
Wales	5	0	5	0	-51	4	4

RISING STARS ON TOP OF THE WORLD

2024 was a sensational year for England U20s.

After winning the U20 Six Nations championship, England's youngsters headed to South Africa for the World Rugby U20 Championship, as the 12 best teams in that age group battled it out over five gruelling match days.

England topped their pool with wins against Argentina, Fiji, and hosts South Africa, before beating Ireland in a thrilling semi final.

In the final, England outmuscled France with a ruthless display in Cape Town, as Mark Mapletoft's side clinched a 21-13 win to end the recent French dominance of the competition and seal England's first World Rugby U20 Championship title since 2016.

The future of English rugby is looking very bright indeed.

ENGLAND'S RESULTS AT THE WORLD RUGBY U20 CHAMPIONSHIP

POOL STAGES

England 40-21 Argentina
England 48-11 Fiji
South Africa 12-17 England

POOL PHASE STANDINGS

	P	W	D	D	Pts Diff	Bonus	Pts
England	3	3	0	0	61	2	14
Argentina	3	2	0	1	40	2	10
South Africa	3	1	0	2	26	2	6
Fiji	3	0	0	3	-127	0	0

SEMI FINAL

England 31-20 Ireland

FINAL

England 21-13 France

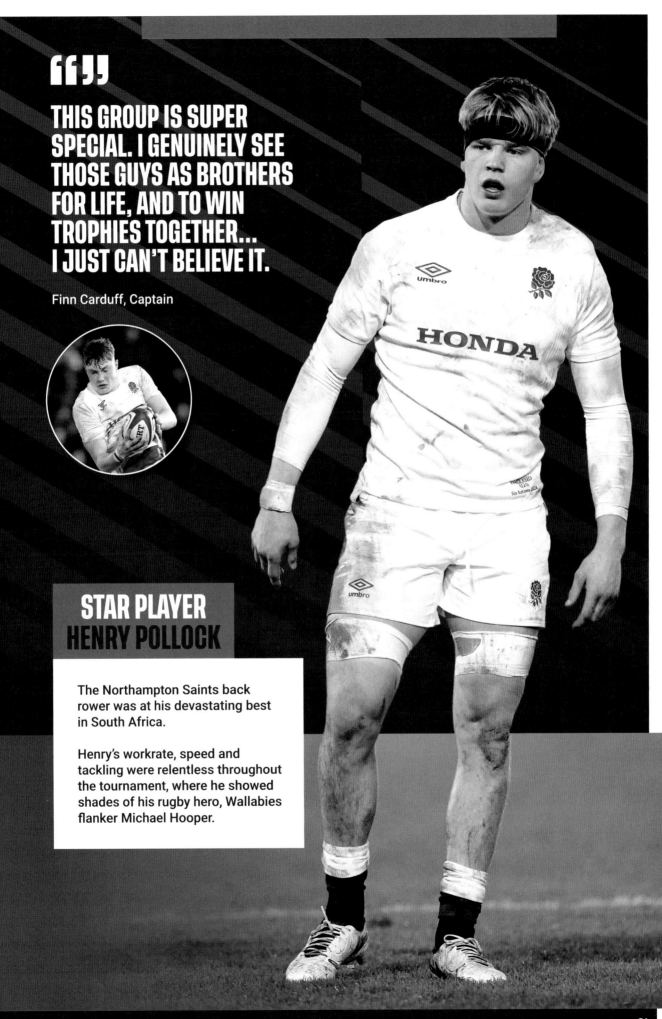

> **"**

THIS GROUP IS SUPER SPECIAL. I GENUINELY SEE THOSE GUYS AS BROTHERS FOR LIFE, AND TO WIN TROPHIES TOGETHER... I JUST CAN'T BELIEVE IT.

Finn Carduff, Captain

STAR PLAYER
HENRY POLLOCK

The Northampton Saints back rower was at his devastating best in South Africa.

Henry's workrate, speed and tackling were relentless throughout the tournament, where he showed shades of his rugby hero, Wallabies flanker Michael Hooper.

DID YOU KNOW?

RED ROSES EDITION

We all know how good the Red Roses are on the pitch, but what about their lives off the pitch?

HERE ARE 10 THINGS YOU MIGHT NOT KNOW ABOUT THE ENGLAND WOMEN'S SQUAD.

1. Abbie Ward gave birth to a beautiful little baby called Hallie in July 2023. seventeen weeks later, she was in the starting line-up for the Red Roses' 2024 Six Nations opener against Italy.

2. Ellie Kildunne isn't just a world-class rugby player; she's also an incredibly talented photographer. Ellie shares her take on everyday life through @elliekfilms on subjects ranging from trips and training to friends and festivals.

3. Emily Scarratt was offered a scholarship to move to the USA at the age of 16 following a tour to New York with her local basketball club, Hinkley and Bosworth, which she turned down. It's safe to say that basketball's loss is rugby's gain!

4. In addition to being one of the game's best scrum halves, Natasha Hunt is also a qualified teacher. Having trained at King Edward's School in Birmingham, she went on to teach PE at Sir Graham Balfour School in Stafford.

5. When she's not throwing pinpoint lineouts or adding to her impressive try-scoring record with Leicester Tigers and the Red Roses, Amy Cokayne dedicates her time to serving as an officer in the Royal Air Force: "I owe a lot to the RAF," Amy explains, "They not only support me as a full-time professional athlete, but they also helped me to find the love of rugby again."

6. Talking of PE teachers... guess who Sadia Kabeya's PE teacher was between the ages of 14-17 at Harris City Academy in Crystal Palace? None other than Saracens and England prop, Bryony Cleall. The pair went on to become England teammates in 2021.

7. From cheering on from the stands to being cheered on from the stands, Jess Breach was a Red Roses superfan growing up, and was there supporting England Women with her family at the 2010, 2014, and 2017 Rugby World Cups.

8. A lot of players have quirky habits and routines, and Zoe Aldcroft is no different. She carries a knitted doll of Jonny Wilkinson in her kit bag at every match: "My friend's gran knitted it for me – he's in Toulon kit – and it comes in my bag to every game."

9. Always one to give back to the community, when the UK went into national lockdown in November 2020, Meg Jones partnered with a sports academy to provide free online fitness sessions to children. Way to go, Meg.

10. One of the game's brightest minds on and off the pitch, Abby Dow is also the holder of a first-class degree in mechanical engineering from one of the world's top universities, Imperial College London.

RED ROSES

MAKE IT 6 IN A ROW

Once again, the Red Roses swept aside all their Six Nations rivals to secure an astonishing sixth straight title. Here's how they did it.

ITALY 0 – 48 ENGLAND

Despite what the final score might suggest, the Red Roses were made to work hard for this result, playing most of the game with 14 players after Sarah Beckett was shown an early red card. The deadlock was eventually broken on the half-hour mark when Hannah Botterman crashed over, and her Bristol Bears teammate Abbie Ward followed that up with another before the break.

No doubt fired up by a lively half-time team talk, England pulled away after the restart, with tries from Marlie Packer, Helena Rowland, Mackenzie Carson, Connie Powell and two from Ellie Kildunne, as the Red Roses got their campaign off to an impressive start.

ENGLAND 46 – 10 WALES

From Parma to Bristol, where England took on Wales in their first home match of the tournament. The Red Roses put on a show in front of 19,705 fans at Ashton Gate, with the forwards doing the damage in the first half as Maud Muir, Hannah Botterman, Zoe Aldcroft and Lark Atkin-Davies all crossed inside the first 40 minutes.

The second half belonged to the backs, though, with Ellie Kildunne posting two tries, including one seemingly impossible acrobatic finish in the corner, and Abby Dow getting her first try of the campaign. Rosie Galligan also got her name on the scoresheet as the Red Roses ran in eight tries for the second game in a row.

SCOTLAND 0 – 46 ENGLAND

After a rest week, England headed north to take on Scotland at the Hive Stadium. England made a blistering start in wet and windy conditions with Amy Cokayne – making her return to Test rugby after a 12-month absence – and Abby Dow both scoring inside 12 minutes. Ellie Kildunne then added a third after a slick kicking move that the Lionesses would have been proud of!

Sadia Kabeya sealed the bonus point shortly after the restart, and that was followed by two tries in six minutes from Jess Breach. Kildunne then bagged her second, and squad captain Marlie Packer sealed the win with a close-range try 10 minutes after coming on as a substitute. Job done in Edinburgh. Next stop: the home of English rugby.

1 TO 100 A day to remember for Maddie Feaunati [left], who won her first England cap, and Marlie Packer [right], who won her 100th.

ENGLAND 88 – 10 IRELAND

The Red Roses returned to Allianz Stadium for the first time since that memorable afternoon in 2023 when they sealed a Grand Slam in front of a record crowd. This time, nearly 50,000 fans piled into Allianz Stadium, and they were treated to another stunning performance as the Red Roses ran in 14 tries against Ireland.

England's back three of Abby Dow, Ellie Kildunne and Jess Breach were at their devastating best, scoring eight tries between them. Meg Jones dotted down two, while Natasha Hunt, Zoe Aldcroft, and Sadia Kabeya also got on the scoresheet, and Maddie Feaunati put the sealing touch on an emphatic win with her first-ever try at international level. What a place to do it!

FRANCE 21 – 42 ENGLAND

Four wins from four, and on to a Grand Slam decider against France in Bordeaux.

Gloucester-Hartpury's forwards got the Red Roses up and running early on with close range scores from Maud Muir and Alex Matthews. France rallied with two tries of their own, but once again, the English pack mauled their way over with two tries in quick succession from Marlie Packer and Amy Cokayne. Meg Jones picked off an intercept and darted over before Alex Matthews sealed the win, as England clinched a sixth straight title and a third Grand Slam in a row against their old rivals, Les Bleus. Way to go, Red Roses!

FINAL STANDINGS

	P	W	L	D	Pts Diff	Bonus	Pts
England	5	5	0	0	229	5	28
France	5	4	1	0	73	3	19
Ireland	5	2	3	0	-71	2	10
Scotland	5	2	3	0	-50	1	9
Italy	5	1	4	0	-74	3	7
Wales	5	1	4	0	-107	1	5

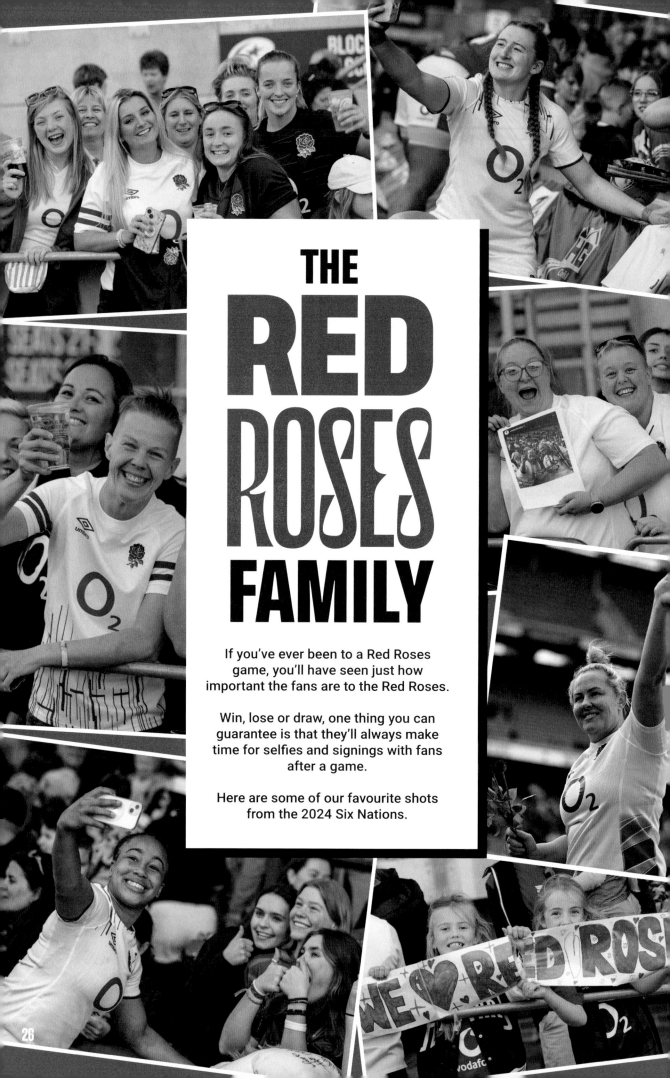

THE RED ROSES FAMILY

If you've ever been to a Red Roses game, you'll have seen just how important the fans are to the Red Roses.

Win, lose or draw, one thing you can guarantee is that they'll always make time for selfies and signings with fans after a game.

Here are some of our favourite shots from the 2024 Six Nations.

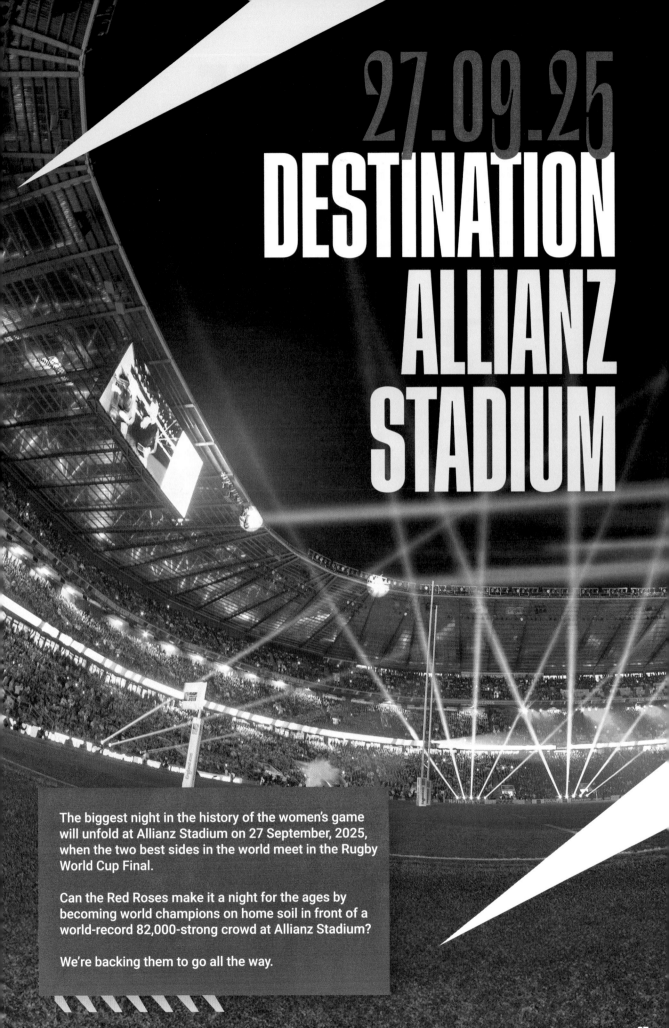

27.09.25
DESTINATION ALLIANZ STADIUM

The biggest night in the history of the women's game will unfold at Allianz Stadium on 27 September, 2025, when the two best sides in the world meet in the Rugby World Cup Final.

Can the Red Roses make it a night for the ages by becoming world champions on home soil in front of a world-record 82,000-strong crowd at Allianz Stadium?

We're backing them to go all the way.

SPOT THE DIFFERENCE

England Rugby fans are some of the most eagle-eyed out there, but can you spot the five differences between these two pictures from the Guinness Men's Six Nations?

ANSWERS ON PAGE 60

TIME TO THINK OUTSIDE THE BOX

Can you guess the 15 players from the emojis below?
Each pair of emojis gives you a clue to part - or all - of a current England
player's surname. If you get stuck, try using the clues underneath each emoji
set, or the player profiles at the back of this book to help you.

Good luck!

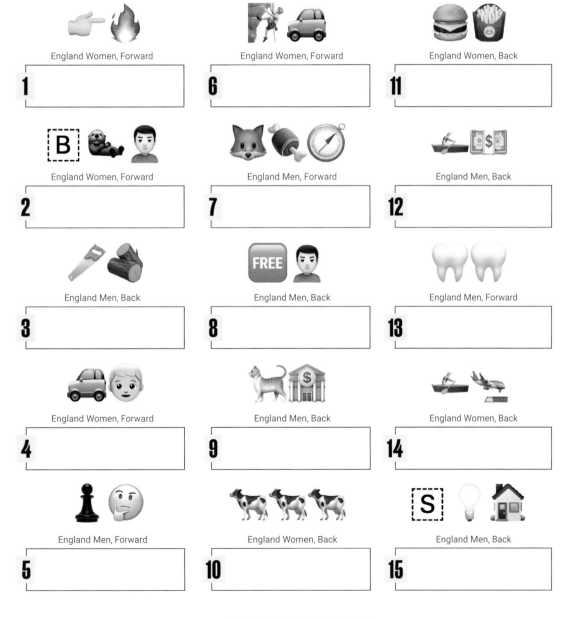

England Women, Forward

1

England Women, Forward

6

England Women, Back

11

England Women, Forward

2

England Men, Forward

7

England Men, Back

12

England Men, Back

3

England Men, Back

8

England Men, Forward

13

England Women, Forward

4

England Men, Back

9

England Women, Back

14

England Men, Forward

5

England Women, Back

10

England Men, Back

15

ANSWERS ON PAGE 61

THE WORLD AT HER FEET

RED ROSES

ELLIE KILDUNNE WAS NAMED 2024 SIX NATIONS PLAYER OF THE CHAMPIONSHIP WITH AN INCREDIBLE SERIES OF PERFORMANCES FOR THE RED ROSES.

WANT TO KNOW WHY? JUST TAKE A LOOK AT SOME OF THESE MINDBOGGLING STATS.

OUT OF THE 180+ PLAYERS WHO FEATURED IN THE TOURNAMENT, ELLIE WAS RANKED NO. 1 FOR:

POINTS SCORED	TRIES SCORED	METRES CARRIED	METRES GAINED	LINE BREAKS
45	9	869	676	13

QUITE SIMPLY, AMAZING.

Ellie Kildunne
England vs France
Twickenham Stadium
29.04.2023

OLYMPIC DREAMS

Red Roses pair Meg Jones and Ellie Kildunne swapped 15s for 7s in the summer of 2024 to pursue their dreams of representing Team GB at the Paris Olympics.

GB beat Ireland and South Africa, with Meg and Ellie providing plenty of eye-catching moments at a packed-out Stade de France but finished second in their pool behind Australia. In the knock-out stages, GB narrowly lost to the USA and then China, but bounced back in the 7th place play-off with a 28-12 win against Ireland.

Needless to say, we couldn't be prouder of them.

Both Meg and Ellie have since switched back to 15s and are raring to go ahead of a massive season with the Red Roses.

England Rugby

SUMMER SERIES

After kicking off their Summer Tour with a convincing 17-52 win against Japan in Tokyo, England Men headed south to face New Zealand in a hotly anticipated two-Test Series against the All Blacks.

THERE'S NO CEILING TO HOW GOOD THIS TEAM CAN BE.

Jamie George speaking to BBC Sport at Eden Park.

NEW ZEALAND 16-15 ENGLAND

England came within a score of recording their first victory in New Zealand since 2003 in the Series opener in Dunedin. Fin Baxter made his Test debut when he came off the bench to replace Harlequins teammate, Joe Marler, as both sides created plenty of chances in the first half.

With the scores locked at 10-10, Immanuel Feyi-Waboso scored a superb try after the restart, but Damian McKenzie's 65th-minute penalty edged New Zealand back in front, which proved to be the decisive score as the hosts held out for the win.

NEW ZEALAND 24-17

Most of England's squad hadn't even been born the last time New Zealand lost at Eden Park [in 1994 against France], but England again pushed the All Blacks all the way in a thrilling match in Auckland.

Marcus Smith unleashed two pin-point cross-field kick assists for Immanuel Feyi-Waboso and Tommy Freeman as England played some eye-catching rugby, but a Beauden Barrett-inspired All Blacks side eventually prevailed.

Despite losing the Series 2-0, the boys put in two spirited performances, and our youngsters gained some invaluable experience in one of the toughest environments in world rugby.

SUPER DAN

A SPECIAL MENTION FOR DAN COLE, WHO CAME OFF THE BENCH IN THE 2ND TEST TO BECOME ENGLAND MEN'S MOST-CAPPED FORWARD OF ALL TIME. WHAT AN ACHIEVEMENT!

BACK-TO-BACK

Gloucester-Hartpury won the 2023/24 Premiership Women's Rugby title to become just the second side to secure back-to-back titles.

The Cherry and Whites, boasting several England internationals, backed up their first-place finish in the regular season with a brave performance in the final, overturning a 17-7 half-time deficit to beat Bristol Bears 36-24 at Sandy Park.

SAINTS GLORY

Northampton Saints sealed their first Premiership title in 10 years, giving club legend Courtney Lawes the perfect send-off at Allianz Stadium.

Saints had a one-man advantage for most of the match after an early red card for Beno Obano, but had to withstand a ferocious Bath fightback in the second half. The men from Franklin's Gardens eventually held out to win a nail-biting encounter 25-21 to become Premiership champions for the second time in their history.

"OF COURSE

I MEANT IT"

As bizarre assists go, Joe Marler's assist for Courtney Lawes' try against Japan at the Rugby World Cup 2023 is right up there with the best.

With England breaking into the Japan 22, George Ford's deflected pass ricocheted off Joe's head and miraculously looped its way into Courtney's arms, who glided under the posts to score.

The header assist was so good, in fact, that Joe's favourite football team, Brighton & Hove Albion, decided to send him a personalised shirt with 'Marler 1' on the back.

In an interview after the game, Joe cheekily claimed that his headed assist was deliberate. We believe you, Joe!

SPOT THE BALL

Can you spot the real ball?

ANSWER ON PAGE 61

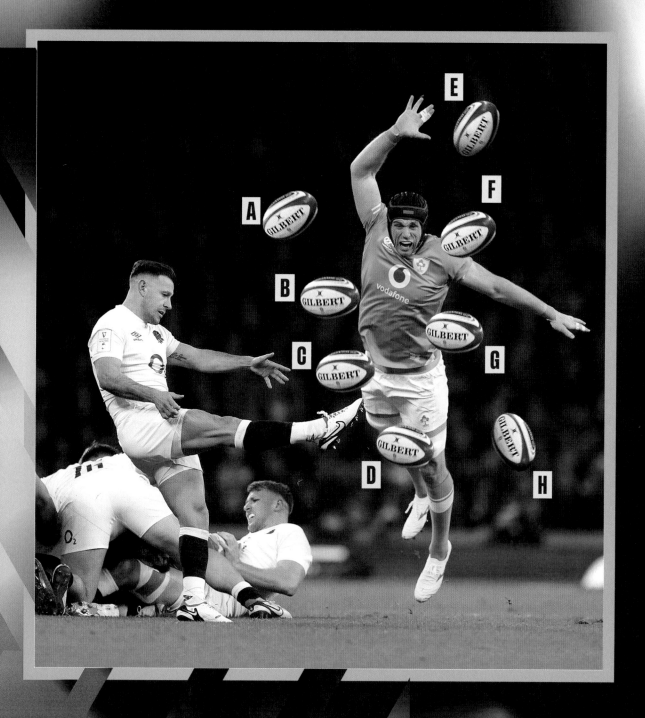

GRASSROOTS HEROES

BEN AND WILLIAM'S BIG DAY

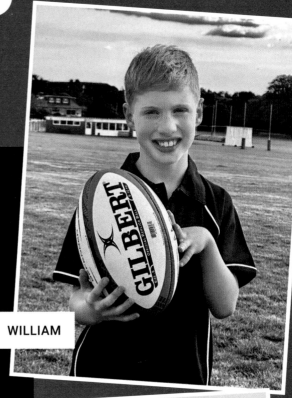

WILLIAM

BEN

Two very excited young rugby players from Wimbledon RFC were selected to be the official ball carriers for the Gallagher Premiership Final at Twickenham. Ben Lort-Phillips, who has autism, and William Pangbourne, who had a stroke as a baby which limits the use of one side of his body, joined the club's 'Inclusives' squad. This team welcomes children with autism, learning difficulties, and a wide range of disabilities, encouraging them to learn a whole new set of skills from their love of rugby. This can often lead to team members graduating through to mainstream teams, joining tours, festivals and finding firm friends. Ben and William now play for the club's Under 10s and just loved meeting star players and being centre stage in a packed-out stadium.

BRILLIANT BELLA

When faced with the prospect of having to leave Weston Rugby Club because there weren't enough girls to make up a team, Bella decided to start recruiting.

"In rugby, there's a stage where the girls and boys don't play together anymore," Bella's mum explained. The choice at Weston was basically start a team or leave, because there wasn't a girls' section. Bella didn't want to leave. She wanted to carry on playing where her family had played before, so she took it upon herself to start building a team."

Fast-forward to today, and thanks to Bella's incredible recruitment efforts, Weston Roses now has a thriving 75-strong girls section.

So, as a special thank you, we organised a little trip for Bella to meet her favourite player, Holly Aitchison, and have a guided tour around the Bristol Bears Performance Centre. Oh, and we also threw in four tickets to watch the Red Roses take on the Black Ferns at Allianz Stadium in September.

Nothing less than Bella deserves for her fantastic work helping to grow the girls' rugby section at Weston!

T1 RUGBY

If you enjoy playing Touch Rugby, there's an exciting new non-contact game coming your way: T1 Rugby.

Launched this year by World Rugby, T1 Rugby is all about fun, fitness and inclusion. A game for everyone, played by anyone.

In a nutshell, it's similar to Touch or Tag, but also includes some of the unique characteristics of traditional 15-a-side rugby, like scrums, lineouts, kicking, and the breakdown.

The game is played on a half-sized pitch with seven players on each side. Substitutes are rolling and unlimited, and games are 20 minutes long (10 minutes per half).

It's simple and fun to play and it doesn't matter how old you are or your level of ability, anyone can play!

SEARCH 'T1 RUGBY' TO FIND OUT MORE AND GET INVOLVED.

RWC 2025 IN NUMBERS

400,000
THE TOTAL NUMBERS OF MATCH TICKETS THAT WILL GO ON SALE.

82,000
THE CAPACITY OF ALLIANZ STADIUM, THE VENUE FOR THE FINAL.

58,498
THE CURRENT WORLD ATTENDANCE FOR A WOMEN'S RUGBY MATCH.

95
THE % OF THE POPULATION WITHIN TWO HOURS TRAVEL TIME OF A MATCH VENUE.

36
THE NUMBER OF DAYS FROM THE FIRST GAME TO THE LAST.

30
THE COST IN £ FOR A FAMILY OF FOUR TO WATCH THE OPENING MATCH.

16
THE NUMBER OF TEAMS AT RWC 2025.

10
THIS WILL BE THE 10TH WOMEN'S RUGBY WORLD CUP.

6
THE NUMBER OF TIMES ENGLAND HAVE FINISHED AS RUNNERS-UP.

10
THE NUMBER OF HOST VENUES.

2
THE NUMBER OF TIMES ENGLAND HAVE WON.

1
THE RED ROSES' CURRENT WORLD RANKING

HERE ARE SOME KEY DATES IN 2024, AS THE COUNTDOWN BEGINS TO RUGBY WORLD CUP 2025.

22 AUGUST
One year to go to.

24 SEPTEMBER
Opening and final match tickets presale for all fans registered on the Rugby World Cup 2025 website.

27 SEPTEMBER - 12 OCTOBER
WXV (also the last Women's RWC 2025 qualifiers).

OCTOBER 2024
Pool phase draw. Match schedule announcement. Tickets go on sale for all matches.

2024 MATCH

ENGLAND MEN'S RESULTS

2023 SUMMER INTERNATIONALS

WALES 20 – 9 ENGLAND
Saturday, 5 August
CARDIFF

ENGLAND 19 – 17 WALES
Saturday, 12 August
LONDON

IRELAND 29 – 10 ENGLAND
Saturday, 19 August
DUBLIN

ENGLAND 22 – 30 FIJI
Saturday, 26 August
LONDON

2023 MEN'S RUGBY WORLD CUP

POOL STAGES

ENGLAND 27 – 10 ARGENTINA
Saturday, 9 September
MARSEILLE

ENGLAND 34 – 12 JAPAN
Sunday, 17 September
NICE

ENGLAND 71 – 0 CHILE
Saturday, 23 September
LILLE

ENGLAND 18 – 17 SAMOA
Saturday, 7 October
NICE

KNOCKOUT STAGES

ENGLAND 30 – 24 FIJI
Sunday, 15 October
MARSEILLE QUARTER FINAL

ENGLAND 15 – 16 SOUTH AFRICA
Saturday, 21 October
PARIS SEMI FINAL

ENGLAND 26 – 23 ARGENTINA
Friday, 27 October
PARIS BRONZE FINAL

2024 MEN'S SIX NATIONS

ITALY 24 – 27 ENGLAND
Saturday, 3 February
ROME

ENGLAND 16 – 14 WALES
Saturday, 10 February
LONDON

SCOTLAND 30 – 21 ENGLAND
Saturday, 24 February
EDINBURGH

ENGLAND 23 – 22 IRELAND
Saturday, 9 March
LONDON

FRANCE 33 – 31 ENGLAND
Saturday, 16 March
LYON

2024 SUMMER SERIES

JAPAN 17 – 52 ENGLAND
Saturday, 22 June
TOKYO

NEW ZEALAND 16 – 15 ENGLAND
Saturday, 6 July
DUNEDIN

NEW ZEALAND 24 – 17 ENGLAND
Saturday, 13 July
AUCKLAND

RESULTS

ENGLAND WOMEN'S RESULTS

AUTUMN INTERNATIONALS

ENGLAND 50 – 24 CANADA
Saturday, 23 September
EXETER

ENGLAND 29 – 12 CANADA
Saturday, 30 September
LONDON

WXV 2023

ENGLAND 42 – 7 AUSTRALIA
Saturday, 21 October
WELLINGTON

ENGLAND 45 – 12 CANADA
Friday, 27 October
DUNEDIN

ENGLAND 33 – 12 NEW ZEALAND
Saturday, 4 November
AUCKLAND

2024 WOMEN'S SIX NATIONS

ITALY 0 – 48 ENGLAND
Sunday, 24 March
PARMA

ENGLAND 46 – 10 WALES
Saturday, 30 March
BRISTOL

SCOTLAND 0 – 46 ENGLAND
Saturday, 13 April
EDINBURGH

ENGLAND 88 – 10 IRELAND
Saturday, 20 April
LONDON

FRANCE 21 – 42 ENGLAND
Saturday, 27 April
BORDEAUX

SQUAD PROFILES

England Rugby

FORWARDS

FIN BAXTER

Position: Prop
Age: 22
Height: 1.70m
Weight: 105kg
Caps: 2
Club: Harlequins

DAN COLE

Position: Prop
Age: 37
Height: 1.91m
Weight: 124kg
Caps: 115
Club: Leicester Tigers

CHANDLER CUNNINGHAM-SOUTH

Position: Flanker
Age: 21
Height: 1.96m
Weight: 120kg
Caps: 7
Club: Harlequins

ALEX COLES

Position: Lock
Age: 24
Height: 1.95m
Weight: 117kg
Caps: 7
Club: Northampton Saints

BEN CURRY

Position: Flanker
Age: 26
Height: 1.85m
Weight: 106kg
Caps: 5
Club: Sale Sharks

TOM CURRY

Position: Flanker
Age: 26
Height: 1.85m
Weight: 109kg
Caps: 53
Club: Sale Sharks

THEO DAN

Position: Hooker
Age: 23
Height: 1.80m
Weight: 100kg
Caps: 14
Club: Saracens

ALEX DOMBRANDT

Position: No. 8
Age: 27
Height: 1.91m
Weight: 118kg
Caps: 17
Club: Harlequins

CHARLIE EWELS

Position: Lock
Age: 29
Height: 1.97m
Weight: 112kg
Caps: 31
Club: Bath

BEN EARL

Position: Flanker
Age: 26
Height: 1.84m
Weight: 107kg
Caps: 33
Club: Saracens

JAMIE GEORGE

Position: Hooker
Age: 33
Height: 1.83m
Weight: 107kg
Caps: 93
Club: Saracens

JOE HEYES

Position: Prop
Age: 25
Height: 1.89m
Weight: 126kg
Caps: 7
Club: Leicester Tigers

MARO ITOJE

Position: Lock
Age: 29
Height: 1.95m
Weight: 118kg
Caps: 84
Club: Saracens

JOE MARLER

Position: Prop
Age: 33
Height: 1.83m
Weight: 120kg
Caps: 95
Club: Harlequins

GEORGE MARTIN

Position: Lock
Age: 23
Height: 1.98m
Weight: 118kg
Caps: 15
Club: Leicester Tigers

GABRIEL OGHRE

Position: Hooker
Age: 26
Height: 1.78m
Weight: 102kg
Caps: 0
Club: Bristol Bears

BEVAN RODD

Position: Prop
Age: 23
Height: 1.83m
Weight: 117kg
Caps: 7
Club: Sale Sharks

ETHAN ROOTS

Position: Flanker
Age: 26
Height: 1.88m
Weight: 110kg
Caps: 4
Club: Exeter Chiefs

SAM UNDERHILL

Position: Flanker
Age: 27
Height: 1.86m
Weight: 103kg
Caps: 38
Club: Bath

WILL STUART

Position: Prop
Age: 27
Height: 1.89m
Weight: 127kg
Caps: 41
Club: Bath

BACKS

JOE CARPENTER

Position: Full back
Age: 22
Height: 1.82m
Weight: 89kg
Caps: 0
Club: Sale
Sharks

IMMANUEL FEYI-WABOSO

Position: Wing
Age: 21
Height: 1.80m
Weight: 94kg
Caps: 6
Club: Exeter
Chiefs

FRASER DINGWALL

Position: Centre
Age: 25
Height: 1.83m
Weight: 96kg
Caps: 0
Club:
Northampton
Saints

GEORGE FURBANK

Position: Full back
Age: 27
Height: 1.82m
Weight: 87kg
Caps: 11
Club:
Northampton
Saints

OLLIE LAWRENCE

Position: Centre
Age: 24
Height: 1.82m
Weight: 99kg
Caps: 27
Club: Bath

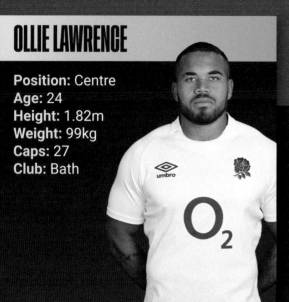

TOMMY FREEMAN

Position: Full back
Age: 23
Height: 1.88m
Weight: 92kg
Caps: 11
Club: Northampton Saints

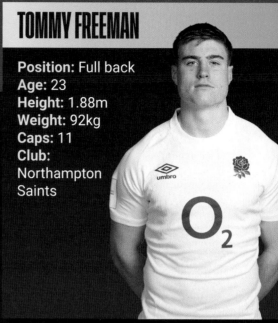

ALEX MITCHELL

Position: Scrum half
Age: 27
Height: 1.80m
Weight: 81kg
Caps: 18
Club: Northampton Saints

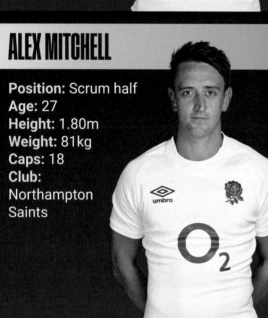

LUKE NORTHMORE

Position: Centre
Age: 27
Height: 1.88m
Weight: 98kg
Caps: 0
Club: Harlequins

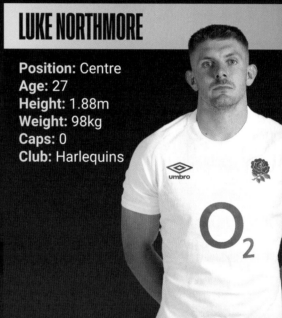

HARRY RANDALL

Position: Scrum half
Age: 26
Height: 1.72m
Weight: 72kg
Caps: 7
Club: Bristol Bears

TOM ROEBUCK

Position: Wing
Age: 23
Height: 1.90m
Weight: 95kg
Caps: 1
Club: Sale Sharks

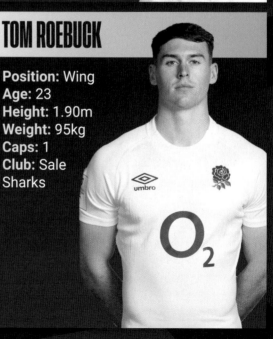

HENRY SLADE

Position: Centre
Age: 31
Height: 1.91m
Weight: 96kg
Caps: 65
Club: Exeter Chiefs

OLLIE SLEIGHTHOLME

Position: Centre
Age: 24
Height: 1.79m
Weight: 96kg
Caps: 2
Club: Northampton Saints

FIN SMITH

Position: Fly half
Age: 22
Height: 1.80m
Weight: 88kg
Caps: 5
Club: Northampton Saints

MARCUS SMITH

Position: Fly half
Age: 25
Height: 1.76m
Weight: 82kg
Caps: 35
Club: Harlequins

BEN SPENCER

Position: Scrum half
Age: 31
Height: 1.78m
Weight: 83kg
Caps: 5
Club: Bath

FREDDIE STEWARD

Position: Full back
Age: 23
Height: 1.96m
Weight: 104kg
Caps: 34
Club: Leicester Tigers

FORWARDS

ZOE ALDCROFT

Position: Lock
Age: 27
Height: 1.81m
Weight: 85kg
Caps: 53
Club: Gloucester-Hartpury

SARAH BERN

Position: Prop
Age: 26
Height: 1.70m
Weight: 91kg
Caps: 61
Club: Bristol Bears

LARK ATKIN-DAVIES

Position: Hooker
Age: 29
Height: 1.62m
Weight: 85kg
Caps: 57
Club: Bristol Bears

SARAH BECKETT

Position: No. 8
Age: 25
Height: 1.78m
Weight: 96kg
Caps: 35
Club: Gloucester-Hartpury

HANNAH BOTTERMAN

Position: Prop
Age: 25
Height: 1.58m
Weight: 103kg
Caps: 47
Club: Bristol Bears

MACKENZIE CARSON

Position: Prop
Age: 26
Height: 1.70m
Weight: 90kg
Caps: 16
Club: Gloucester -Hartpury

KELSEY CLIFFORD

Position: Prop
Age: 22
Height: 1.68m
Weight: 105kg
Caps: 8
Club: Saracens

AMY COKAYNE

Position: Hooker
Age: 27
Height: 1.67m
Weight: 86kg
Caps: 74
Club: Leicester Tigers

LIZ CRAKE

Position: Prop
Age: 29
Height: 1.78m
Weight: 96kg
Caps: 2
Club: Ealing Trailfinders

MADDIE FEAUNATI

Position: Flanker
Age: 22
Height: 1.75m
Weight: 85kg
Caps: 5
Club: Exeter Chiefs

ROSIE GALLIGAN

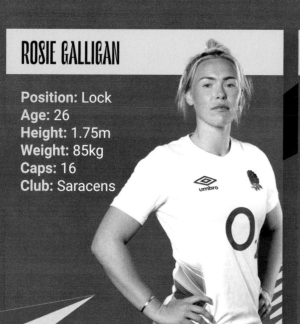

Position: Lock
Age: 26
Height: 1.75m
Weight: 85kg
Caps: 16
Club: Saracens

SADIA KABEYA

Position: Flanker
Age: 22
Height: 1.70m
Weight: 84kg
Caps: 18
Club:
Loughborough
Lightning

ALEX MATTHEWS

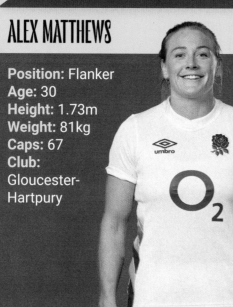

Position: Flanker
Age: 30
Height: 1.73m
Weight: 81kg
Caps: 67
Club:
Gloucester-
Hartpury

MAUD MUIR

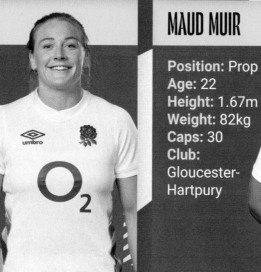

Position: Prop
Age: 22
Height: 1.67m
Weight: 82kg
Caps: 30
Club:
Gloucester-
Hartpury

CATHERINE O'DONNELL

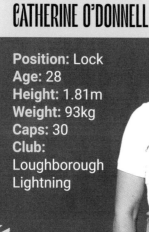

Position: Lock
Age: 28
Height: 1.81m
Weight: 93kg
Caps: 30
Club:
Loughborough
Lightning

MARLIE PACKER

Position: Flanker
Age: 34
Height: 1.65m
Weight: 78kg
Caps: 104
Club: Saracens

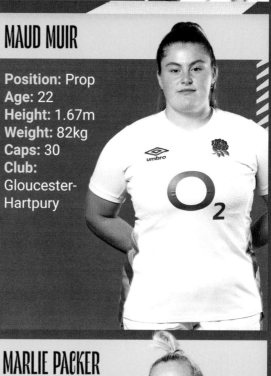

CONNIE POWELL

Position: Hooker
Age: 23
Height: 1.65m
Weight: 88kg
Caps: 19
Club: Harlequins

MORWENNA TALLING

Position: Flanker
Age: 21
Height: 1.85m
Weight: 84kg
Caps: 13
Club: Sale Sharks

ABBIE WARD

Position: Lock
Age: 31
Height: 1.81m
Weight: 78kg
Caps: 65
Club: Bristol Bears

BACKS

HOLLY AITCHISON

Position: Fly half
Age: 26
Height: 1.75m
Weight: 69kg
Caps: 30
Club: Bristol Bears

JESSICA BREACH

Position: Wing
Age: 26
Height: 1.68m
Weight: 73kg
Caps: 38
Club: Saracens

ABIGAIL DOW

Position: Wing
Age: 26
Height: 1.68m
Weight: 72kg
Caps: 45
Club: Ealing Trailfinders

ZOE HARRISON

Position: Fly half
Age: 26
Height: 1.73m
Weight: 73kg
Caps: 49
Club: Saracens

NATASHA HUNT

Position: Scrum half
Age: 35
Height: 1.65m
Weight: 67kg
Caps: 72
Club: Gloucester-Hartpury

TATYANA HEARD

Position: Centre
Age: 29
Height: 1.64m
Weight: 75kg
Caps: 22
Club: Gloucester-Hartpury

MEGAN JONES

Position: Centre
Age: 27
Height: 1.60m
Weight: 67kg
Caps: 21
Club: Leicester Tigers

ELLIE KILDUNNE

Position: Full back
Age: 24
Height: 1.76m
Weight: 68kg
Caps: 43
Club: Harlequins

CLAUDIA MACDONALD

Position: Wing
Age: 28
Height: 1.67m
Weight: 65kg
Caps: 32
Club: Exeter Chiefs

LUCY PACKER

Position: Scrum half
Age: 24
Height: 1.61m
Weight: 55kg
Caps: 21
Club: Harlequins

HELENA ROWLAND

Position: Centre
Age: 24
Height: 1.68m
Weight: 66kg
Caps: 29
Club: Loughborough Lightning

EMILY SCARRATT

Position: Centre
Age: 34
Height: 1.81m
Weight: 77kg
Caps: 11
Club: Loughborough Lightning

ELLA WYRWAS

Position: Scrum half
Age: 25
Height: 1.60m
Weight: 63kg
Caps: 6
Club: Saracens

ANSWERS

THE AMAZING RUGBY WORDSEARCH

Y	F	H	K	D	L	L	A	D	N	A	R	Y	R	R	A	H	R
A	L	L	I	A	N	Z	S	T	A	D	I	U	M	L	K	G	O
Y	S	I	X	N	A	T	I	O	N	S	E	A	X	A	T	L	F
B	Z	F	L	U	D	F	I	T	O	R	S	L	J	N	L	S	F
Q	R	O	M	A	U	D	M	U	I	R	F	L	D	I	S	E	S
T	E	E	L	M	O	F	I	X	R	E	S	I	E	F	B	U	I
M	C	R	D	E	V	G	R	A	A	I	T	L	B	I	O	E	D
A	T	H	K	R	T	Y	P	E	S	E	A	S	M	M	N	I	E
S	I	D	L	U	O	I	R	O	D	W	D	T	N	E	U	M	P
C	A	N	E	B	H	S	O	T	R	D	I	A	N	S	S	I	L
O	J	A	L	A	O	D	E	E	A	D	U	D	P	U	P	V	S
T	X	L	Z	C	T	G	N	A	T	U	M	I	O	X	O	I	E
H	A	R	T	W	I	C	M	E	R	H	E	E	D	B	I	N	N
B	V	E	R	L	E	A	R	T	Y	T	V	R	I	P	N	Q	O
S	I	D	O	F	B	M	A	R	C	U	S	S	M	I	T	H	J
K	E	N	P	C	E	R	H	B	E	B	A	F	H	G	I	B	G
A	R	U	H	L	M	A	X	B	M	E	J	N	U	B	E	S	E
T	O	S	Y	E	L	O	C	N	A	D	G	J	K	G	E	T	M

WHO AM I?

Tom Curry

SPOT THE DIFFERENCE

TIME TO THINK OUTSIDE THE BOX

1. 🔫🔥 **Bern** England Women, Forward
2. Ⓑ 🦫👨 **Botterman** England Women, Forward
3. 🪓🤛 **Carpenter** England Men, Back
4. 🚗👶 **Carson** England Women, Forward
5. ♟️👴 **Chessum** England Men, Forward
6. 🎏🚗 **Clifford** England Women, Forward
7. 🦊🧭 **Cunningham-South** England Men, Forward
8. FREE👨 **Freeman** England Men, Back
9. 🐈🏛️ **Furbank** England Men, Back
10. 🐕🐕 **Heard** England Women, Back
11. 🍔🍟 **Macdonald** England Women, Back
12. 🛶💲 **Roebuck** England Men, Back
13. 🦷🦷 **Roots** England Men, Forward
14. 🚣✈️ **Rowland** England Women, Back
15. Ⓢ 🏠 **Sleightholme** England Men, Back

SPOT THE BALL

BALL 'B'

FIND MARCUS

Can you spot England Men's fly-half Marcus Smith in the crowd?